FILL YOUR HORN WITH OIL AND GO!

Dr. Gregory A. Uvieghara

Copyright © 2012 by DR. GREGORY A. UVIEGHARA

FILL YOUR HORN WITH OIL AND GO!
by DR. GREGORY A. UVIEGHARA

Printed in the United States of America

ISBN 9781622302918

All rights reserved solely by the author. The author guarantees all contents are original and do not infringe upon the legal rights of any other person or work. No part of this book may be reproduced in any form without the permission of the author. The views expressed in this book are not necessarily those of the publisher.

Unless otherwise indicated, all scriptures quotations in this book are from the New King James Versions of the Bible, Copyright 1982 by Thomas Nelson, Inc. Used by permission. All rights reserved.
Scripture quotations marked (AMP) are taken form the Amplified Bible , Copyright 1954, 1958, 1962, 1964, 1965, 1987 by the Lockman Foundation. Used by permission. Scripture quotations marked Weymouth are from the Weymouth New Testament, Richard Francis Weymouth, 1912. Public domain in the United States

The World –Penetrating Word Sword is a trademark of All Nations For Christ Ministries, Inc., registered with the U. S. Patent and Trademark Office and therefore may not be duplicated.

www.xulponpress.com

ALL NATIONS FOR CHRIST MINISTRIES

42172 ANGELS PEAK COURT

Murrieta, CA 92562, U.S.A.

DEDICATION

This book is dedicated to Prophetess Jean Perez, my spiritual mother, who prophesied that I should get all my books out to the Body of Christ, and to Sister Catherine Hardy, a pioneer director of ALL NATIONS FOR CHRIST MINISTRIES, for her self-less and untiring support for the vision of the ministry.

CONTENTS

CHAPTER 1
BACKGROUND 9

CHAPTER 2
INTRODUCTION 11

CHAPTER 3
SYMBOLS: 'HORN' AND 'OIL' 28

CHAPTER 4
FILL YOUR HORN 45

CHAPTER 5
FILL YOUR HORN WITH OIL 55

CHAPTER 6
FILL YOUR HORN WITH OIL AND GO 76

APPENDIX I
A SINNER'S PRAYER TO RECEIVE JESUS CHRIST AS SAVIOR 87

APPENDIX II
A BELIEVER'S PRAYER TO RECEIVE THE BAPTISM IN THE HOLY SPIRIT WITH THE EVIDENCE OF SPEAKING IN OTHER TONGUES 89

Chapter 1
BACKGROUND

☦

"Fill your horn with oil, and go!" Those words leaped at me! In August, 2000, I was flying on a Japan Airlines plane to Tokyo for a preaching engagement, minding my own business. There was a Japanese man sitting on my right and a Japanese woman sitting on my left. Cruising at more than 30,000 feet in the air, I was preparing my message *"The Spirit of David"* from **1 SAM. 17**. I then felt led by the Lord to read the chapter preceding **1 SAM. 17**, in order to get a better perspective of the **1 SAM. 17** context. As I read:

1 SAM. 16:1

1 Now the Lord said to Samuel, "How long will you mourn for Saul, seeing I have rejected him from reigning over Israel? FILL YOUR HORN WITH OIL, AND GO; I am sending you to Jesse the Bethlehemite. For I have provided Myself a king among his sons."

the words **"Fill your horn with oil, and go"** leaped at me from the Bible. Within the twinkling of an eye, I got a message: **"Fill your horn with oil and go!"** In less than a minute after that, a series of supporting scriptures and revelations lined themselves up in my heart. I first preached the message in the Japanese preaching engagement I was flying to, as part of my *"Altering the Japanese Spiritual Climate"* series. Further meditations and refinements of the message have led to this book.

The way I stumbled on this golden nugget is a perfect example of what two ministers wrote and said a couple of years ago. One minister, J. Sidlow Baxter, once wrote *"I would remind fellow-preachers that the greatest sermons usually come when we are not looking for sermons but are studying the word of God for the sake of its own vital truth."* Another minister, Kenneth Hagin, once said: *"Sometimes the greatest leadings we ever have is when we are unconsciously led by the Spirit of God. Sometimes we are looking for something spectacular and miss the supernatural."* Now, I am confident that the Spirit of the Lord led me, even though at that time I was not conscious of it. Looking back, I now see that I was being unconsciously led by the Holy Spirit to the revelation for this book.

Chapter 2
INTRODUCTION

†

What led to **1 SAM 16:1**? Saul had just been rejected from being the king of Israel. In **1 SAM. 13**, we read:

1 SAM. 13:1-14

1 Saul reigned one year; and when he had reigned TWO YEARS over Israel,

2 Saul chose for himself three thousand men of Israel. Two thousand were with Saul in Michmash and in the mountains of Bethel, and a thousand were with Jonathan in Gibeah of Benjamin. The rest of the people he sent away, every man to his tent.

3 And Jonathan attacked the garrison of the Philistines that was in Geba, and the Philistines heard of it. Then Saul blew the trumpet throughout all the land saying, "Let the Hebrews hear!"

4 Now all Israel heard it said that Saul had attacked a garrison of the Philistines, and that Israel had also become an abomination to the Philistines. And the people were called together to Saul at Gilgal.

5 Then the Philistines gathered together to fight with Israel, thirty thousand chariots and six thousand horsemen, and people

as the sand which is on the seashore in multitude. And they came up and encamped in Michmash, to the east of Beth Aven.

6 When the men of Israel saw that they were in danger (for the people were distressed), then the people hid in caves, in thickets, in rocks, in holes, and in pits.

7 And some of the Hebrews crossed over the Jordan to the land of Gad and Gilead. As for Saul, he was still in Gilgal, and all the people followed him trembling.

8 Then he waited seven days, according to the time set by Samuel. But Samuel did not come to Gilgal; and the people were scattered from him.

9 So Saul said, "Bring a burnt offering and peace offerings HERE TO ME." And HE OFFERED THE BURNT OFFERING.

10 Now it happened, as soon as he had finished presenting the burnt offering, that Samuel came; and Saul went out to meet him, that he might greet him.

11 And Samuel said, "What have you done?" Saul said, "When I saw that the people were scattered from me, and that you did not come within the days appointed, and that the Philistines gathered together at Michmash,

12 "then I said, 'The Philistines will now come down on me at Gilgal, and I have not made supplication to the Lord.' Therefore I felt compelled, and offered a burnt offering."

13 And Samuel said to Saul, "You have done foolishly. YOU HAVE NOT KEPT THE COMMANDMENT OF THE LORD

YOUR GOD, WHICH HE COMMANDED YOU. FOR NOW THE LORD WOULD HAVE ESTABLISHED YOUR KINGDOM OVER ISRAEL FOREVER.

14 "BUT NOW YOUR KINGDOM SHALL NOT CONTINUE. THE LORD HAS SOUGHT FOR HIMSELF A MAN AFTER HIS OWN HEART, AND THE LORD HAS COMMANDED HIM TO BE COMMANDER OVER HIS PEOPLE, BECAUSE YOU HAVE NOT KEPT WHAT THE LORD COMMANDED YOU."

So we see from **1 SAM. 13:1**, that Saul had fallen from grace in just two years!

Saul's Fall

Saul failed two tests before God rejected him. The basic issue in the two tests was a simple matter of obedience. When God tells you to do something, just do it. Don't ask questions; don't do it half-heartedly; don't do part of it and leave part of it undone.

The *first test* Saul failed is depicted in **1 SAM. 13** above. Samuel had told Saul in **1 SAM. 10**.

1 SAM. 10:8

8 "You shall go down before me to Gigal; and SURELY I WILL COME DOWN TO YOU TO OFFER burnt offerings and make

sacrifices of peace offerings. Seven days YOU SHALL WAIT, TILL I COME TO YOU and show you what you should do.

Samuel's instruction in **1 SAM. 10:8** was very clear. First, he assured Saul *"surely I will come down to you."* Therefore, unless he heard otherwise from Samuel, Saul should have rested on the assurance that Samuel had given him which was that he would unfailingly come to Gilgal. Second, Samuel made it clear that he (*Samuel*) was the one to offer the sacrifice: *"I will come ... to offer burnt offerings and make sacrifices of peace offerings."* Third, Samuel made it very clear: *"you shall wait, till I come to you."*

But what did Saul do? He waited for seven days, and because the people were running away, he thought he could just go through the motions of performing a sacrifice and everything would be all right. The people were running away because the Philistines were coming. The people of Israel were scattered and Saul just said to himself [*author's paraphrase*] *"well, since Samuel is not here, I will just perform this sacrifice and solve all my problems."* But by doing that he exalted himself to be a priest. He was called to be a king and not a priest. In contrast, Samuel was both a prophet and a priest, but he never exalted himself to be a king, even though he was judge over Israel. Samuel always stood in the office to which he was called.

(Tongues & Interpretation: *It is a very dangerous thing to step into offices you are not called to.* In the Old Testament, you could lose your life immediately, but in the New Testament because of the grace of God and the blood of Jesus that has been shed, your judgment may be delayed. But if you do not correct yourself, judgment will eventually catch up with you. For example, William Branham was an American prophet who was prominent in the healing revival of the 1950's and the 1960's. William Branham died prematurely. A prominent prophet believes that he shortened his life because instead of remaining in the prophetic office to which he was called, he tried to also be a teacher.)

The rebuke Saul received from Samuel in **1 SAM. 13:13**: *"you have not kept the commandment of the Lord your God, which he commanded you"* shows Saul failed his **first obedience test**.

The *"straw that broke the camel's back"* was when Saul failed his **second obedience test**: he disobeyed God's divine command to inflict complete judgment on Amalek as shown in **1 SAM. 15**.

1 SAM. 15:1-23
1 Samuel also said to Saul, "The Lord sent me to anoint you king over His people, over Israel. Now therefore, heed the voice of the words of the Lord.
2 "Thus says the Lord of hosts: 'I will punish Amalek for what he did to Israel, how he ambushed him on the way when he came up from Egypt.
3 'Now go and attack Amalek, and UTTERLY DESTROY ALL THAT THEY HAVE, and do not spare them. But kill both man

and woman, infant and nursing child, ox and sheep, camel and donkey.' "

4 So Saul gathered the people together and numbered them in Telaim, two hundred thousand foot soldiers and ten thousand men of Judah.

5 And Saul came to a city of Amalek, and lay in wait in the valley.

6 Then Saul said to the Kenites, "Go, depart, get down from among the Amalekites, lest I destroy you with them. For you showed kindness to all the children of Israel when they came up out of Egypt." So the Kenites departed from among the Amalekites.

7 And Saul attacked the Amalekites, from Havilah all the way to Shur, which is east of Egypt.

8 He also took Agag king of the Amalekites alive, and utterly destroyed all the people with the edge of the sword.

9 BUT SAUL AND THE PEOPLE SPARED AGAG AND THE BEST OF THE SHEEP, THE OXEN, THE FATLINGS, THE LAMBS, AND ALL THAT WAS GOOD, AND WERE UNWILLING TO UTTERLY DESTROY THEM. BUT EVERYTHING DESPISED AND WORTHLESS, THAT THEY UTTERLY DESTROYED.

10 Now the word of the Lord came to Samuel, saying,

11 "I greatly regret that I have set up Saul as king, for he has turned back from following Me, and HAS NOT PERFORMED MY COMMANDMENTS." And it grieved Samuel, and he cried out to the Lord all night.

12 So when Samuel rose early in the morning to meet Saul, it was told Samuel, saying, "Saul went to Carmel, and indeed, he set up a monument for himself; and he has gone on around, passed by, and gone down to Gilgal."

13 Then Samuel went to Saul, and Saul said to him, "Blessed are you of the Lord! I HAVE PERFORMED THE COMMANDMENT OF THE LORD."

14 But Samuel said, "WHAT THEN IS THIS BLEATING OF THE SHEEP IN MY EARS, AND THE LOWING OF THE OXEN WHICH I HEAR?"

15 And Saul said, "They have brought them from the Amalekites; for the people spared the best of the sheep and the oxen, to sacrifice to the Lord your God; and the rest we have utterly destroyed."

16 Then Samuel said to Saul, "Be quiet! And I will tell you what the Lord said to me last night." And he said to him, "Speak on."

17 So Samuel said, "When you were little in your own eyes, were you not head of the tribes of Israel? And did not the Lord anoint you king over Israel?

18 "Now the Lord sent you on a mission, and said, 'GO, AND UTTERLY DESTROY THE SINNERS, THE AMALEKITES, and fight against them until they are consumed.'

19 "WHY THEN DID YOU NOT OBEY THE VOICE OF THE LORD? Why did you swoop down on the spoil, and do evil in the sight of the Lord?"

20 And Saul said to Samuel, "BUT I HAVE OBEYED THE VOICE OF THE LORD, and gone on the mission on which the Lord sent me, and brought back Agag king of Amalek; I have utterly destroyed the Amalekites.

21 "But the people took of the plunder, sheep and oxen, the best of the things which should have been utterly destroyed, to sacrifice to the Lord your God in Gilgal."

22 So Samuel said:

> "HAS THE LORD AS GREAT DELIGHT IN BURNT OFFERINGS AND SACRIFICES,
> AS IN OBEYING THE VOICE OF THE LORD?
> BEHOLD, TO OBEY IS BETTER THAN SACRIFICE,
> AND TO HEED THAN THE FAT OF RAMS.
> FOR REBELLION IS AS THE SIN OF WITCHCRAFT,
> AND STUBBORNNESS IS AS INIQUITY AND IDOLATRY.
> BECAUSE YOU HAVE REJECTED THE WORD OF THE LORD,
> HE ALSO HAS REJECTED YOU FROM BEING KING."

The divine commandment was clear. God said: *"Go to Amalek and destroy everything you find there."* But what did Saul do? He destroyed some things but he left some things undestroyed. And guess what things he left undestroyed? The worthy things; the worthless things, he totally destroyed. God rejected Saul as king because he failed to utterly destroy the Amalekites; instead he chose to keep the best of the best for himself. To cover up his mess, he sacrificed to God in a misguided attempt to make God overlook his disobedience. But God did not want his sacrifice; God wanted his obedience.

Just as our Lord Jesus Christ was not fooled by the rich young man's flattery in **MATT. 19:16**, *"GOOD Teacher,"* Samuel was not fooled by Saul's flattery in **1 SAM. 15:13**, *"BLESSED are you of the Lord!"* Although Saul was swelling with self-congratulation in **1 SAM. 15:13**, *"I have performed the commandment of the Lord,"* Samuel saw through his hypocrisy. The evidence, *"bleating of the sheep in my ears, and the lowing of the oxen which I hear,"* in **1 SAM. 15:14** was very compelling. The evidence clearly contradicted Saul's claim that he had obeyed the Lord. After his hypocrisy was exposed, Saul then attempted to shift the blame to the people in **1 SAM. 15:15**: *"for the people spared the best of the sheep and the oxen"*. But his attempt to shift the blame for his disobedience failed since the "buck always stops" with the king. (In fact, blame-shifting has never worked with God and will never work with God. Ask Adam who tried to shift blame to Eve directly and to God indirectly by telling God in **GEN. 3:12**: *"The woman whom You gave to be with me, she gave me of the tree, and I ate."* Or ask Aaron who tried to shift the blame for constructing the golden calf to the people, by telling Moses in **EXOD. 32:23**: *"For they (the people) said to me, 'Make us gods that shall go before us;' "*) Further, Saul's claim in **1 SAM. 15:15**: *"for the people spared the best of the sheep and* *the oxen, to sacrifice to the Lord your God"* did not fool Samuel. Samuel's response in **1 SAM. 15:22**: *"behold, to obey is better than sacrifice"* shows that no amount of sacrifice can ever be a substitute for simple obedience. In **DEUT. 10;17**, Moses told the people of Israel: *"For the Lord your God ... shows no partiality nor takes a bribe."* In other words, you can never bribe God with your sacrifice for Him to overlook your disobedience.

In **ISAIAH**, we see God's total discontent with any attempt to manipulate him through sacrifices.

ISA. 1: 11 – 17:

11 "TO WHAT PURPOSE *IS* THE MULTITUDE OF YOUR SACRIFICES TO ME?"
Says the Lord.
"I have had enough of burnt offerings of rams
And the fat of fed cattle.
I do not delight in the blood of bulls,
Or of lambs or goats.

12 "When you come to appear before Me,
Who has required this from your hand,
To trample My courts?

13 Bring no more futile sacrifices;
Incense is an abomination to Me.

The New Moons, the Sabbaths, and the calling of assemblies—

I cannot endure iniquity and the sacred meeting.

14 Your New Moons and your appointed feasts

My soul hates;

They are a trouble to Me,

I am weary of bearing *them*.

15 When you spread out your hands,

I will hide My eyes from you;

Even though you make many prayers,

I will not hear.

Your hands are full of blood.

16 "Wash yourselves, make yourselves clean;

Put away the evil of your doings from before My eyes.

Cease to do evil,

17 Learn to do good;

Seek justice,

Rebuke the oppressor;

Defend the fatherless,

Plead for the widow.

I am alarmed when I see Christians try to manipulate God through fasting. The prophet Isaiah warned against this very wrong practice of fasting in order to manipulate God. Check your motives if you ever find yourself interrogating God like the people of Israel in **ISA. 58:3**:

'Why have we fasted,' they say, 'and You have not seen?
Why have we afflicted our souls, and You take no notice?'

I personally know a prophet who I believe died prematurely because he engaged in the dangerous practice of trying to manipulate God through fasting. Before getting to know him well, I was always impressed with his long fasts and consistent fasted life. But after getting close to him I realize that even when he knew what God's word clearly said about a particular issue, he would try to use long fasts to alter God's will. What I saw from afar when I did not know him well was totally different from what I observed after getting close to him.

What was Saul's motive? Covetousness. Although Saul claimed the sheep and oxen were saved for sacrifice, the truth of the matter was that Saul coveted the spoil as revealed in Samuel's question in **1 SAM. 15:19**: *"Why did you swoop down on the spoil?"* (Saul's covetousness was similar to that of Achan in **JOSH. 7**, whose coveting of a Babylonian garment, two hundred shekels of silver, and a wedge of gold (**JOSH. 7:21**) led to the Ai debacle.)

From verses 13 to 21 of **1 SAM. 15**, Saul, after Samuel had exposed his sin, had several opportunities to repent and to at least postpone judgment. But Saul, in his futile attempt at self-justification, kept on arguing with Samuel. Samuel then had no alternative but to pronounce God's final judgment in **1 SAM. 15:23**: *"He (God) also has rejected you from being king."*

Passive Obedience Versus Active Obedience

It is interesting to note that Saul was tested in two aspects of obedience: *passive obedience* and *active obedience*. *Passive obedience* requires you to *do nothing* but *wait*, while *active obedience* requires you to *do something*. *Passive obedience* required Saul to *wait*, to do nothing until God moved: Saul was asked to wait until Samuel (God's representative) showed up to perform the sacrifice in Gilgal (**1 SAM. 10:8**). *Active obedience* required Saul to *do something: to totally destroy* everything in Amalek (**1 SAM. 15:3**). In the case of Gilgal, Saul obeyed until the very last moment when he gave up on Samuel and went ahead to perform the sacrifice himself. In the case of Amalek, Saul only destroyed the *worthless* things, but not everything. Therefore, in both cases, Saul missed God not because he did not obey at all, but because he did not *completely obey*. All this underscores the fact that *incomplete obedience* is *disobedience* as far as God is concerned.

Samuel's Dejection

Samuel became dejected after he pronounced God's judgment on Saul.

1 SAM. 15:35
35 And Samuel went no more to see Saul until the day of his death. Nevertheless, SAMUEL MOURNED FOR SAUL,

Samuel was crying, weeping to God, mourning. You probably have been in circumstances like this where a man that is called by God misses God, through sexual sin, through love of money or through pride. And he destroys his own life and ministry. It breaks your heart; and you mourn. You are then in the position of Samuel who, probably, was asking himself, *"how can this man anointed by God to be the king over Israel squander the anointing just like that?"*

A few years ago, I gave a short exhortation at a bible school graduation. The pastor was sitting behind me while I was on the pulpit. In the middle of my speech, the Holy Spirit interrupted me, the hand of the Lord came upon me, the Holy Spirit arrested my tongue and I could not speak in English. I then had an utterance in tongues. The interpretation was: *"Don't take your ministry lightly. Take heed that you fulfill it."* In a sense, it was similar to what Paul wrote to Archippus in **COL. 4:17** : *"Take heed to the ministry which you have received in the Lord, that you may fulfill it."* The pastor, who was sitting behind me, said: *"Good word."* I thought the message was for the graduating students but I found out later that it was for the pastor. A few months later, because the pastor was stubborn, arrogant and would not listen to anybody, he lost his church and ministry. I found out later that the word I gave him was similar to one that a South African prophet had earlier given him. (Sometimes people feel that ministers fall only through sexual sin. But pride is probably the number one way a minister can fall.) This pastor said he heard directly from God, and that he did not need to take counsel from anybody. But we know that God can and does talk through people. This pastor fell. One day, he just resigned from the pastoral office and the church split and broke down. That very day, after the pastor resigned, I went home, mourning and crying, and said: *"God, what is this? Please, let me never get into a position where I will fall like this man."* The last thing I heard was that his wife had a stroke; they probably opened the door for the devil through their disobedience.

We see here that Samuel was disheartened because he knew what the anointing meant. He knew the anointing that was on Saul, and therefore the gravity of Saul's fall. It was more than a personal loss; it was a national loss of gigantic proportions. Samuel knew what kingdom business meant. Remember Samuel was the last judge or spiritual governor of Israel. Before Saul, there were no kings in Israel. Israel just had people like Samuel who were judges. Some were prophets and judges like Samuel, while some were priests and judges like Eli; not all judges were prophets. The judges were like spiritual kings with spiritual leadership over Israel. Samuel was like a spiritual watchman over Israel. Therefore, spiritually, he understood the significance of what had happened to Saul; that broke his heart. It was like seeing Samson throw away his anointing because of women (**JUDG. 16:17**) or Esau selling his birthright for a bowl of porridge (**GEN. 25:34**).

Several years ago, some prominent TV evangelists fell in the U.S. It broke the hearts of many Christians. I was doing my doctorate in Electronics at the time at the University of California, Berkeley. After these men fell, I vividly remember being mocked by one of my Berkeley classmates who I had been witnessing to. While the world was laughing, the church was crying. I know a certain Nigerian minister who I believe was an apostle-evangelist. I have no doubt in my mind that he certainly stood in those two offices, mightily anointed by God and well-known all over the world. This Nigerian minister missed God through spiritual pride and he died prematurely, breaking many hearts. With these present-day examples I have just cited, you can better relate to the spiritual significance of Saul's fall and why Samuel was so dejected.

In the midst of all his dejection, God spoke directly from heaven: **"Fill your horn with oil and go."** God was telling Samuel to stop crying over spilt milk. You must know that there are certain things you cannot resurrect. Once these things are dead, they are dead. When God says something is final, it is final. In essence, God told Moses (**DEUT. 3:26**): *"Don't cry to me anymore, you are not going into the promised land. That's it. It is done. End of negotiation. The negotiation table is closed. Don't discuss this with me anymore."* But if you keep on pushing, you can come to a point of serious danger when you get to the point of no-return. When God said something is over, it is over. God told Joshua (**JOSH. 1:2**): *"Moses, my servant, is dead."* When God says someone is dead, that person is dead. You don't need a doctor to take his pulse and try to determine if the person is brain-dead or just partially dead. Similarly, when God says an issue is over, it is over.

Look at Balaam in **NUM. 22 & 23**. God had told him not to go to Balak. However, Balaam said: *"let me go and pray again and see if God wants me to go or not."* But God had already told him not to go. When you keep on pushing, you will eventually push beyond the point of no return. You will then come to a point that God will not speak to you anymore. Rather, the devil will then accommodate you, making you think that God has changed His mind. Beyond the point of no return, you open yourself up for satanic deception. Therefore, Samuel had enough spiritual common sense to cease pressing Saul's case after God had told him that He had rejected Saul.

My paraphrase of what God told Samuel is: *"Enough, I have rejected Saul. It is a final matter. No more discussion. Saul has been rejected. He is no longer going to be king of Israel. He may still physically be sitting on the throne, but I have lifted my anointing from him. "* Although Samuel perfectly understood why God had rejected Saul, Saul's fall weighed very heavily on his heart. Saul's fall was probably the biggest disappointment Samuel faced in his ministry. Therefore, a defining moment in Samuel's ministry was when, at his zero hour, as he lay prostrate on the floor mourning for Saul, a voice rang from heaven: **"Fill your horn with oil and go!"**

Chapter 3
SYMBOLS: 'HORN' AND 'OIL'

✝

Four articles of the Old Testament prophet carried symbolic meanings: *'staff'*, *'cloak'*, *'horn'*, and *'oil'*. Imagine an Old Testament prophet having a *'cloak'* on, and holding a *'staff'* in his right hand and a *'horn'* of *'oil'* in his left hand. With this vivid picture firmly fixed in your mind, let us now examine the symbolic meaning of each article.

'Staff'

The prophet's *'rod'* or *'staff'* was a scepter, a symbol of authority that symbolized power, authority or dominion. The prophet carried the *staff* as an emblem of authority just like a king held his scepter as an emblem of authority. It was therefore sometimes used as a point of contact for miracles. The clearest example of this is the case of Moses. After Moses was commissioned to go and deliver the people of Israel from Egyptian bondage, Moses' rod became God's rod:

EXOD. 4:20
20 And Moses took the ROD OF GOD in his hand.

As a point of contact, this staff was used to perform miracles, signs and wonders. Let us look at a couple of scriptures on how the rod or staff was used to perform miracles.

EXOD. 7:10

10 Aaron cast down his ROD before Pharaoh and before his servants, and it became a serpent.

EXOD. 7:12

12 But Aaron's ROD swallowed up their rods.

EXOD. 7:20

20 And Moses and Aaron did so, just as the Lord commanded. So he lifted up the ROD and struck the waters that were in the river, in the sight of Pharaoh and in the sight of his servants. And all the waters that were in the river were turned to blood.

EXOD. 8:5

5 Then the Lord spoke to Moses, "Say to Aaron, 'Stretch our your hand with your ROD over the streams, over the rivers, and over the ponds, and cause frogs to come up on the land of Egypt.' "

EXOD. 8:16

16 So the Lord said to Moses, "Say to Aaron, 'Stretch out your ROD, and strike the dust of the land, so that it may become lice throughout all the land of Egypt.' "

EXOD. 9:23

23 And Moses stretched out his ROD toward heaven; and the Lord sent thunder and hail, and fire darted to the ground. And the Lord rained hail on the land of Egypt.

EXOD. 10:13

13 So Moses stretched out his ROD over the land of Egypt, and the Lord brought an east wind all that day and all that night. When it was morning, the east wind brought the locusts.

EXOD. 14:16

16 "But lift up your ROD, and stretch our your hand over the sea and divide it. And the children of Israel shall go on dry ground through the midst of the sea."

EXOD. 17:5-6

5 And the Lord said to Moses, "Go on before the people, and take with you some of the elders of Israel. Also take in your hand your ROD with which you struck the river, and go.
6 "Behold, I will stand before you there on the rock in Horeb; and you shall strike the rock, and water will come out of it, that the people may drink." And Moses did so in the sight of the elders of Israel.

EXOD. 17:9,11

9 And Moses said to Joshua, "Choose us some men and go out, fight with Amalek. Tomorrow I will stand on the top of the hill with the ROD OF GOD in my hand."

11 And so it was, when Moses held up his hand, that Israel prevailed; and when he let down his hand, Amalek prevailed.

Another example of the prophet's *'staff'* was in the case of Elisha. In the following verses, we see Elisha instructing Gehazi, his servant, to use his *'staff'* to perform a miracle.

2 KINGS 4:25-29

25 And so she departed, and went to the man of God *(Elisha)* at Mount Carmel. So it was, when the man of God saw her afar off, that he said to his servant Gehazi, "Look, the Shunammite woman!

26 "Please run now to meet her, and say to her, 'Is it well with you? Is it well with your husband? Is it well with the child? " And she answered, "It is well."

27 Now when she came to the man of God at the hill, she caught him by the feet, but Gehazi came near to push her away. But the man of God said, "Let her alone; for her soul is in deep distress, and the Lord has hidden it from me, and has not told me."

28 So she said, "Did I ask a son of my lord? Did I not say, 'Do not deceive me'?"

29 Then he said to Gehazi, "Get yourself ready, and take **MY STAFF** in your hand, and be on your way. If you meet anyone, do not greet him; and if anyone greets you, do not answer him; but **LAY MY STAFF ON THE FACE OF THE CHILD.**"

'Cloak'

The prophet's *'cloak'*, mantle or outer overcoat represented his ministerial office, his anointing, rank, and ministerial burden or responsibility. Remember Elijah threw his *'cloak'* on Elisha, symbolizing that Elijah would shortly pass the baton to the next generation through Elisha?

1 KINGS 15-16, 19

15 Then the Lord said to him *(Elijah)*: "Go, return on your way to the Wilderness of Damascus; and when you arrive, anoint Hazael as king over Syria.

16 "Also you shall anoint Jehu the son of Nimshi as king over Israel. And **ELISHA** the son of Shaphat of Abel Meholah **YOU SHALL ANOINT AS PROPHET IN YOUR PLACE.**

19 So he departed from there, and found Elisha the son of Shaphat, who was plowing with twelve yoke of oxen before him, and he was with the twelfth. Then **ELIJAH PASSED BY HIM AND THREW HIS MANTLE** *(CLOAK)* **ON HIM.**

Elijah used his mantle as an instrument for performing miracles.

1 KINGS 2:8

8 Now Elijah took his MANTLE, ROLLED IT UP, AND STRUCK THE WATER; AND IT WAS DIVIDED THIS WAY AND THAT, so that the two of them crossed over on dry ground.

At the moment Elijah was raptured, his mantle fell on Elisha indicating that Elijah's mantle of authority was being placed on the younger Elisha's shoulders.

1 KINGS 2:9-14

9 And so it was, when they had crossed over, that Elijah said to Elisha, "Ask! What may I do for you, before I am taken away from you?" Elisha said, "Please let a double portion of your spirit be upon me."
10 So he said, "You have asked a hard thing. Nevertheless, if you see me when I am taken from you, it shall be so for you; but if not, it shall not be so."
11 Then it happened, as they continued and talked, that suddenly a chariot of fire appeared with horses of fire, and separated the two of them; and Elijah went up by a whirlwind into heaven.
12 And Elisha saw it, and he cried out, "My father, my father, the chariot of Israel and its horsemen" So he saw him no more. And he took hold of his own clothes and tore them into two pieces.

13 He also took up the MANTLE OF ELIJAH THAT HAD FALLEN FROM HIM, and went back and stood by the bank of Jordan.

Like Elijah, Elisha also used his mantle as an instrument for performing miracles.

1 KINGS 2:13
13 HE ALSO TOOK UP THE MANTLE OF ELIJAH THAT HAD FALLEN FROM HIM, AND STRUCK THE WATER, and said, "Where is the Lord God of Elijah?" And when HE ALSO HAD STRUCK THE WATER, IT WAS DIVIDED THIS WAY AND THAT; and Elisha crossed over.

Ministers, who are sensitive, can perceive the mantles on other ministers.

1 KINGS 2:15
15 Now WHEN THE SONS OF THE PROPHETS who were from Jericho SAW HIM, they said, "THE SPIRIT OF ELIJAH RESTS ON ELISHA."

The declaration of the sons of the prophets, *"the spirit of Elijah rests on Elisha",* indicates that they perceived the transfer of Elijah's mantel to Elisha which occurred in **1 KINGS 2:13**.

The woman with the issue of blood was referring to the mantle (*anointing*) on Jesus when she said:

MARK 5:28

28 ... "If only I may touch his clothes (*cloak or mantle*), I shall be made well."

Physically, she touched Jesus' outer cloak, but spiritually, she touched his mantle or made a demand on His anointing.

Before ministering, I sometimes sense my ministerial anointing as a *'cloak'* around me. In general, a minister may sometimes sense his ministerial anointing as a *cloak*. The higher the anointing, the heavier the *cloak* feels.

'Horn'

There are two ways the *'horn'* is used in the Old Testament. In the first way, *'horn'* is used to represent *'strength'*. This is because in the Hebrew language, intellectual or theological concepts are expressed by concrete terms. *'Horn'*, a concrete term, is used to represent *'strength'*, a theological concept. A horn is that hard projection attached to the heads of goats, sheep, or cattle that is used as an attacking weapon. Therefore, *'horn'* is used to represent *'strength'* or *'vigor'*.

PSALM 18:2, PSALM 75:10, PSALM 89:17,24, PSALM 92:10, PSALM 112:9, PSALM 148:14 & LUKE 1:67-69 refer to *'horn'* in this first respect of it being a representation of *'strength'*.

PSALM 18:2

2 The Lord is my rock and my fortress and my deliverer;
My God, my STRENGTH, in whom I will trust;
My shield and the HORN of my salvation, my stronghold.

PSALM 75:10

10 "All the HORNS of the wicked I will also cut off,
But the HORNS of the righteous shall be exalted."

PSALM 89:17,24

17 For you are the glory of their STRENGTH,
And in Your favor our HORN is exalted.
24 "But My faithfulness and My mercy shall be with him,
And in My name his HORN shall be exalted."

PSALM 92:10

10 But my HORN You have exalted like a wild ox;
I have been anointed with fresh oil.

PSALM 112:9

9 He has dispersed abroad,

He has given to the poor;

His righteousness endures forever;

His HORN will be exalted with honor.

PSALM 148:14

14 And He has exalted the HORN of His people,

The praise of all His saints –

Of the children of Israel,

A people near to Him.

Praise the Lord!

LUKE 1:67-69

67 Now his father Zacharias was filled with the Holy Spirit, and prophesied, saying:

68 "Blessed is the Lord God of Israel, For He has visited and redeemed His people,

69 And has raised up a HORN of salvation for us

In the house of His servant David,

Since *'horn'* symbolizes *'strength'*, *'horn'* is used to represent kingdoms, kings or as a symbol of ruling power in the visions of Daniel.

DANIEL 7:7-8, 11, 20-21, 24

7 "After this I saw in the night VISIONS, and behold, a fourth beast, dreadful and terrible, exceedingly strong. It had huge

iron teeth; it was devouring, breaking in pieces, and trampling the residue with its feet. It was different from all the beasts that were before it, and it had TEN HORNS.

8 "I was considering the HORNS, and there was another HORN, a little one, coming up among them, before whom three of the first HORNS were plucked out by the roots. And there, in this HORN, were eyes like the eyes of a man, and a mouth speaking pompous words.

11 "I watched then because of the sound of the pompous words which the HORN was speaking;
I watched till the beast was slain, and its body destroyed and given to the burning flame.

20 "and the TEN HORNS that were on its head, and the other HORN which came up, before which three fell, namely, that HORN which had eyes and a mouth which spoke pompous words, whose appearance was greater than his fellows.

21 "I was watching; and the same HORN was making war against the saints, and prevailing against them,

24 The TEN HORNS ARE TEN KINGS
Who shall arise from this kingdom.
And another shall rise after them;
He shall be different from the first ones,
And shall subdue three kings.

FILL YOUR HORN WITH OIL AND GO!

DANIEL 8:3-9, 12, 16-17, 19-21

3 Then I lifted my eyes and saw, and there, standing beside the river, was a ram which had TWO HORNS, and the TWO HORNS were high; but one was higher than the other, and the higher one came up last.

4 I saw the ram pushing westward, northward, and southward, so that no animal could withstand him; nor was there any that could deliver from his hand, but he did according to his will and became great.

5 And as I was considering, suddenly a male goat came from the west, across the surface of the whole earth, without touching the ground; and the goat had a notable HORN between his eyes.

6 Then he came to the ram that had TWO HORNS, which I had seen standing beside the river, and ran at him with furious power.

7 And I saw him confronting the ram; he was moved with rage against him, attacked the ram, and broke his TWO HORNS. There was no power in the ram to withstand him, but he cast him down to the ground and trampled him; and there was no one that could deliver the ram from his hand.

8 Therefore the male goat grew very great; but when he became strong, the large HORN was broken, and in place of it four notable ones came up toward the four winds of heaven.

9 And out of one of them came a little HORN which grew exceedingly great toward the south, toward the east, and toward the Glorious Land.

12 Because of transgression, an army was given over to the HORN to oppose the daily sacrifices; and he cast truth down to the ground. He did all this and prospered.

16 And I heard a man's voice between the banks of the Ulai, who called, and said, "Gabriel, make this man understand the vision."
17 So he came near where I stood, and when he came I was afraid and fell on my face; but he said to me, "Understand, son of man, that the vision refers to the time of the end."
19 And he said, "Look, I am making known to you what shall happen in the latter time of the indignation; for at the appointed time the end shall be.
20 "The ram which you saw, having the TWO HORNS – THEY ARE THE KINGS OF MEDIA AND PERSIA.
21 "And the male goat is the kingdom of Greece. The LARGE HORN THAT IS BETWEEN ITS EYES IS THE FIRST KING."

According to the verses 20 & 21 above, the angel Gabriel explained to Daniel that the *'horns'* he saw in the visions represented kings and kingdoms. *'Horns'* representing kings derives from the fact that *'horn'* is used to represent *'strength'*.

While in the first way the *'horn'* is used is to represent *'strength'*, in the second way, the *'horn'* was used to carry the prophet's anointing oil. The horns of dead goats, sheep or cattle were sawed off and used as flasks for carrying anointing oil. When God told Samuel *"Fill your horn with oil and go"*, He was referring to the *'horn'* in this second respect. Another example of this is in:

1 KINGS 1:39

39 Then Zadok the priest took a HORN of oil from the tabernacle and anointed Solomon.

So we know that *'horn'* represents strength. But the *'horn'* is used in a different sense in **1 SAM. 16**: as a symbol representing a carrier of God's glory.

'Oil'

Throughout the Bible, *'oil'* represents the Holy Ghost. In the Old Testament, the anointing oil was sprinkled on or poured on the heads of those God set apart for service to typify God's anointing on them to carry out certain tasks. The anointing is an act of dedication and consecration. It implies on the part of the one anointed an unconditional and full surrender to God of his hands to work, his feet to walk, his eyes to see, his lips to speak, his ears to hear for Him and Him alone, and his entire body to be the temple of the Holy Spirit. The first example of the anointing *oil* being used to anoint people for God's service was when Moses anointed Aaron and his sons as priests.

EXODUS 29:7,21

7 "And you (Moses) shall take the ANOINTING OIL, POUR IT ON HIS HEAD, and anoint him (Aaron)."

21 "And you shall take some of the blood that is on the altar, and some of the ANOINTING OIL, AND SPRINKLE IT ON AARON AND ON HIS GARMENTS, ON HIS SONS AND ON THE GARMENTS OF HIS SONS WITH HIM; and he and his garments shall be hallowed, his sons and his sons' garments with him."

LEVITICUS 8:12

12 And HE (Moses) POURED SOME OF THE ANOINTING OIL ON AARON'S HEAD AND ANOINTED HIM, TO CONSECRATE HIM.

Prophets poured the anointing *oil* on individuals to anoint them as kings. The first king of Israel, Saul, was anointed by Samuel in this manner.

1 SAMUEL 10:1

1 Then SAMUEL TOOK A FLASK OF OIL AND POURED IT ON HIS (Saul) HEAD, and kissed him and said: "Is it not because the LORD HAS ANOINTED YOU COMMANDER OVER HIS INHERITANCE?"

Similarly, Elisha sent one of the sons of the prophets to anoint Jehu as king.

2 KINGS 5:6

6 Then he arose and went into the house. And he (son of the prophets) POURED THE OIL ON HIS (Jehu) HEAD, and said to him, "Thus says the Lord God of Israel: 'I HAVE ANOINTED YOU KING OVER THE PEOPLE OF THE LORD, OVER ISRAEL.'"

In the New Testament, the anointing *oil* was used to represent the healing anointing. First, Jesus' disciples anointed the sick.

MARK 6:13

13 And they (*the disciples*) cast out many demons, and ANOINTED WITH OIL MANY WHO WERE SICK, AND HEALED THEM.

Second, **JAMES** enjoined believers to anoint the sick with *oil* for divine healing.

JAMES 5:14

14 Is anyone among you sick? Let him call for the elders of the church, and let them pray over him, ANOINTING HIM WITH OIL IN THE NAME OF THE LORD.

Symbols: 'Horn' And 'Oil'

While Moses and Elijah respectively exemplified the prophet's *'staff'* and the prophet's *'cloak'*, Samuel exemplified the prophet's *'horn'* and the prophet's *'oil'*. Notice that the *'horn'* represents you. God said: **"Fill your horn"**. Since God said *"your horn,"* the *'horn'* represents you. But the *'oil'* represents the Holy Ghost. So we see here the combination of the divine and the human. Now, the *'oil'* represents the anointing, and the *'horn'* being the vessel for carrying the *'oil'*, represents the carrier of the anointing or the carrier of God's glory. **PSALM 92:10** is a perfect illustration of this.

PSALM 92:10

10 But MY HORN You have exalted like a wild ox; I have been ANOINTED with fresh OIL.

This book essentially illustrates the interplay between these two symbols: *'horn'* (that symbolizes, you, the carrier of God's anointing) and *'oil'* (that symbolizes the anointing). Throughout this book you will see different pictures being painted by the metaphorical use of these two symbols: *'horn'* and *'oil'*.

Chapter 4
FILL YOUR HORN

God told Samuel, *"Fill your horn"*. Why? Because God does not use empty vessels. Throughout the Bible, God makes it clear that for you to be effective in service you have to be filled with Himself, His word, His anointing, His Spirit and His glory. In the parable of the ten virgins (**MATT. 25:1-13**), it was the five virgins who had no *'oil'* in their vessels (*'horns'*) that were called foolish.

Empty Vessels Make The Loudest Noise

An empty vessel makes the loudest noise. That is why, if you are sensitive, you will perceive that those who are empty of the Word sound like *"empty brass or a clanging cymbal"* (**1 COR. 13:1**) when they speak in tongues. You will get a louder noise from striking an empty horn than from striking a horn filled with oil. An empty *'horn'* makes the loudest noise. God does not use empty vessels. God uses vessels that are filled with Him, filled with the Holy Ghost. *'Horns'* who lose God's power and His presence by not spending enough time with the Master are simply noisy and ineffective for the Kingdom. This is even truer for those who are ministers of the Gospel. Ministers who do not spend enough time with the Lord in the Word and in prayer may make the loudest noise and have the most demonstrative outward expressions while preaching, but sound hollow because of their empty *'horns'*. These empty ministers may shout and jump up and down while preaching, but portray a counterfeit anointing because their *'horns'* are empty. They may quote scriptures, even from memory, but it all sounds empty and hollow because, unfortunately, these scriptures are being quoted from a full head rather than from a full heart. Scriptures not quoted from the heart have no impact in the spirit realm. Because words not spoken from the heart have no spiritual impact, God makes statements like:

ISA. 29:13

13 ... "Inasmuch as these people draw near with their MOUTHS And honor Me with their LIPS,

But have removed their HEARTS far from Me,..."

Empty 'Horns' Can't Take Pressure

It is easier to crush an empty *'horn'* than to crush a full one because a full *'horn'* has something on the inside that can withstand the pressure from the outside. In the same way, the devil finds it easier to oppress Christians that are empty. There is a lot of talk these days about *"spiritual warfare"*. But Christians who are full of the Word and the Spirit have less problems with the devil and find it easier to withstand his attacks, when compared to Christians who are empty *'horns'*. Some Christians want to fight spiritual battles without being full of the Holy Ghost. It does not work. If you are empty, you cannot fight spiritual battles. If you are empty, you will be tossed to and fro by the enemy. Only filled vessels can be used by God in fighting spiritual battles. A lot of the oppression and depression Christians have can simply be dealt with if they just keep their *'horns'* full. You don't have to consciously be binding and losing all the time, in a constant state of frenetic spiritual warfare if your *'horn'* is full. Empty *'horns'* crack under pressure because empty *'horns'* can't take pressure.

You "Fill Your Horn"

Today, God is saying the same thing to you that He said to Samuel hundreds of years ago: *you* **"fill your horn"**. Notice that the understood subject here is *'you'*, not the Holy Spirit. The Holy Spirit will help you but it is primarily your duty to see that your **'horn'** is full. The Holy Spirit can never force you to pray or to read your Bible. Remember, the Holy Ghost is a "Helper", not the main doer. Helpers do not take the initiative; doers take the initiative. You take the initiative and then He comes alongside to help. You have a part to play in getting anointed. What would have happened if Samuel had not obeyed God? Samuel's *'horn'* would have remained empty. God would not have sent an angel down from heaven to fill Samuel's *'horn'* for him. In the same way, your *'horn'* remains empty and you remain un-anointed when you fail to yield to the Holy Ghost's promptings to read the Word or to pray. While Samuel had a physical *'horn'* that he had to fill with physical *'oil'*, your *'horn'* is 'you' as a carrier of God's glory that you get filled by spending time in the Word, in fastings, in prayer (especially praying in tongues), and in the presence of the Lord.

Filled to the Extent of Your Capacity

In **LUKE 6:38**, Jesus said: *"For with the same measure that you use, it will be measured back to you."* That is, the Holy Spirit fills your *'horn'* to the extent of the *'horn'* capacity that you provide Him. The Holy Spirit fills your *'horn'* to the extent that your *'horn'* is empty of yourself, the flesh and carnal desires. A perfect illustration of this principle can be found in the case of Elisha's working of a miracle to fill the widow's vessels in **2 KINGS 4**.

2 KINGS 4:1-6
1 A certain woman of the wives of the sons of the prophets cried out to Elisha, saying, "Your servant my husband is dead, and you know that your servant feared the Lord. And the creditor is coming to take my two sons to be his slaves."
2 So Elisha said to her, "What shall I do for you? Tell me, what do you have in the house?" And she said, "Your maidservant has nothing in the house but a jar of oil."
3 Then he said, "Go, borrow vessels from everywhere, from all your neighbors – empty vessels; do not gather just a few.

4 "And when you have come in, you shall shut the door behind you and your sons; then pour it into all those vessels, and set aside the full ones. "

5 So she went from him and shut the door behind her and her sons, who brought the vessels to her; and she poured it out.

6 Now it came to pass, when the vessels were full, that she said to her son, "Bring me another vessel." And he said to her, "THERE IS NOT ANOTHER VESSEL." SO THE OIL CEASED.

Notice that *"the oil ceased"* after the widow's son answered *"There is not another vessel."* In other words, the *'oil'* ceased flowing after there was no more *'horn'* for it to flow into. Why? Because God will not permit His anointing to drop on the floor. Why? Because the God who said *"Do not give what is holy to the dogs; nor cast your pearls before swine ..."* (**MATT. 7:6**) does not violate His own principles. In other words, God does not squander His anointing. Rather, God gives His anointing to those who are hungry and prepared for it. God *"fills your horn"* to the extent that you have created the capacity for Him to fill. Your capacity is a function of the depth of your spiritual hunger, your willingness to be filled and your readiness to suffer the persecutions and trials that go with the anointing. God will not give you more than you have a capacity for. God will not let his anointing fall on the ground. God will not cast his pearls among swine. The Holy Ghost will work through you to the extent that you yield, open up and provide the capacity for Him to work with. It is to the extent that you make yourself a vessel for the Holy Ghost, that He will fill you. Even in praying in tongues, most people do not develop their praying in the spirit because they just stop at the tongues they received as the initial evidence of the baptism in the Holy Ghost. They still pray the same syllables and phrases in tongues over and over again because they have not yet yielded beyond that initial point. They fail to allow the Holy Spirit to fill them to overflowing as they pray in tongues. They refuse to allow the Holy Spirit to expand their prayer language. You should yield more to the Holy Spirit since God fills your *'horn'* to the extent of your capacity.

Are You Filled With the World Or Filled With The Word?

If you are pre-occupied with the world and the flesh, God will not bother with you; God will just leave you alone. To the extent that you have emptied yourself of the world and the flesh, to that extent God **"fills your horn."** Elisha understood this principle perfectly. Hence, he told the widow in **2 KINGS 4:3** *"do not gather just a few"* vessels. It is either she did not take Elisha's admonition very seriously or she failed to completely communicate it to her sons. The latter is likely because she was expecting another empty vessel from her sons after she had poured into the last one when she said: *"Bring me another vessel."* (**2 KINGS 4:6**). Unfortunately, the widow's son answered: *"There is not another vessel."* And *"the oil ceased."* In a similar way, the oil or the anointing has *"ceased"* to flow into *'horns'* (Christians or ministers) who have pre-occupied themselves with the distractions of the flesh and the world and therefore have no more vessels or capacity to receive the anointing from the Lord.

Fasting: Avenue For Emptying 'Horn'

Fasting is a perfect avenue for emptying oneself of spiritual junk, the flesh and the world, thereby creating room for the Holy Ghost. The other side of the coin is that if you don't pray and read the Word while fasting, you are creating room in your *'horn'* for the devil, instead. A Christian who is fasting without praying and reading the Word is engaged in a very dangerous activity: he is opening himself up for demonic influence rather than the Holy Ghost influence. This is because there are no spiritual vacuums and spiritual laws work the same way, whether positively or negatively. In other words, if the spiritual vacuum the Christian creates in his *'horn'* through fasting is not filled with the Word and the anointing, Satan will attempt to fill the vacuum.

Empty 'Horns' Invite Oppression

In fact, empty 'horns' invite demonic oppression which, in extreme cases, can end up in demonic possession. An extreme example of this is the case of the man Jesus mentioned in **MATT. 12**.

MATT. 12:43-45
43 "When an unclean spirit goes out of a man, he goes through dry places, seeking rest, and finds none.

44 "Then he says, 'I will return to my house from which I came.' And when he comes, he finds it EMPTY, swept, and put in order. 45 "Then he goes and takes with him seven other spirits more wicked than himself, and they enter and dwell there, and the last state of that man is worse than the first. ..."

To be an empty *'horn'* is to give an open invitation to the devil. When *"the devil walks about like a roaring lion, seeking whom he may devour"* (**1 PET. 5:14**), he is looking for Christians who are empty *'horns'*. Pulpit ministers are particularly in danger of demonic oppression if they try to function as empty *'horns'*.

The Consequences of Saul's Empty 'Horn'

An extreme example of how an empty *'horn'* invites demonic oppression/possession is illustrated in the story of Saul. After the anointing lifted from Saul, he did not run towards God. Then an evil spirit came and possessed him. Since Saul's *'horn'* was drained of God, an evil spirit took over and filled his *'horn'* instead. Why? Because there are no vacuums in the spirit realm: if God is out, the devil is in. Saul's demonic oppression eventually ended up in demonic possession. Saul was so possessed that he became a ranting mad man who used the entire army of Israel to chase just one man, David! Saul getting David to play soothing music for him (**1 SAM. 16:14-23**) only helped to temporarily lift the influence of the evil spirit but did not fundamentally address the problem at it's root. His use of David's music was a half-hearted measure like half-hearted measures taken by many present-day Christians. These Christians think that listening to Christian music, watching Christian TV and listening to Christian message tapes are substitutes for personal worship, church attendance and Bible study.

The Danger of Samuel's Empty 'Horn'

Why did God halt Samuel? God knew the kind of danger Samuel faced. I once heard Ed Dufresne say: *"Disappointment, if not dealt with, leads to discouragement. Discouragement, if not dealt with, leads to depression. Finally, depression, if not dealt with, leads to oppression."* Therefore, you should nip disappointment in the bud before it progresses to discouragement, depression and finally to oppression. The kind of grief that Samuel was experiencing could lead to demonic oppression, similar to Saul's, if Samuel was not careful. Since the prophetic ministry operates in the spirit realm, a demonically oppressed prophet is the most dangerous prophet. Samuel was empty at this point. Samuel's **'horn'** was empty of the **'oil' of joy.** Samuel stood the risk of being drained completely with his grieving over Saul's failure. Samuel's **'horn'** was now empty due to his grieving. Saul's **'horn'** was broken; Saul's **'oil'** had been poured out of his broken **'horn'**, but Samuel had to move on. Saul was "past tense", but Samuel had to move on into the future. Therefore, God said **"Fill your horn with oil and go".** Since Samuel was the spiritual watchman over Israel, God could not risk him being so pre-occupied with Saul's fall in such a way as to open a door for the devil. So God, in essence, told him: "enough of that; kingdom business must continue; **fill your horn with oil and go."**

>Filled with God! Yes, filled with God!
>Cleansed by the blood of the Lamb, and filled with God!
>Filled with God! Yes, filled with God!
>Emptied of self and the world, and filled with God!

Chapter 5
FILL YOUR HORN WITH OIL

†

In the last chapter, the emphasis was on **"fill your horn"**; that is, you should never be empty but be always full. But full of what? You should be full of the Word and the Holy Spirit. You can tell what you are full of in three ways: by what you think, what you say and what you dream.

What Are You Thinking?

You can tell what you have in your *'horn'* by what you think for **PROV. 23:7** says: *"For as he thinks in his heart so is he"*. If you constantly examine your thoughts, you can tell whether your mind is occupied with the cares of this life, with pleasure or with the Word. Your thoughts do not have to be sinful per se for them to be worthless or injurious to your spiritual growth. For example, I love soccer. Sometimes I catch myself thinking more about soccer than about the Word. What do I then do? I double up on the Scriptures and minimize my time spent surfing the web on soccer. What are you thinking? Do you have thoughts of regret, grief, or disappointment? Then you have tears in your *'horn'* like Samuel had. You should replace the tears in your *'horn'* with the *'oil'* of joy.

What Are You Saying?

You can tell what you have in your *'horn'* by what you say for **MATT. 12:34** says: *"For out of the abundance of the heart the mouth speaks"*. Notice that this scripture is saying that something must be in abundance in your heart for it to come out of your mouth. It is not sufficient for it to just be in your heart; it must be there in abundance. If it is not there in abundance, it will not come out but the moment it becomes abundant in your heart, there is no stopping it spilling over. For the Word to come out of your mouth, a little bit of Word in your heart is insufficient; the Word must be plentiful in your heart. When Satan puts pressure on your *'horn'* during trials does your *'horn'* buckle? Does the pressure crush your *'horn'*? What comes out of your *'horn'* during trials? For the Word to come out of your *'horn'* during trials, the Word must abundantly be in your *'horn'* prior to the trials. You can tell what people are full of by listening to what they say. If they are full of pride, their words will reveal it in many self-centered statements with "I" as the main subject. People can put on masks for a long time, but what is abundantly in their hearts will eventually come out. No matter how hard they try, Jesus said that what they have in their *'horns'* in abundance will eventually spill over the brims of their *'horns'*. If you are angry with someone, you will eventually find yourself muttering under your breath some negative things about that person. (The most embarrassing aspect of unresolved malice is that, while you are sleeping, your spouse may hear you muttering negative things about the person you are angry with!) After analyzing your words, you can then take the required steps to fix the wrong words with the Word.

There is a connection between what you are *thinking*, what you are *saying* and what your **'horn'** becomes. Your **'horn'** eventually becomes what you *dwell on*. What you are *thinking* about is what you have in your **'horn'** and is what you are *believing*. What you are *believing* is what you are *talking* about as what you have in your **'horn'** is spilling over the brim of your **'horn'**. Eventually, your **'horn'** becomes what you are *thinking*, *believing* and *talking* about.

What Are You Dreaming?

You can tell what you have in your **'horn'** by what you dream for **PROV. 5:3** says: *"For a dream comes through much activity"*. Your dream does not only reveal what you have in your **'horn'** but also what the devil is trying to put in your **'horn'**. In my dreams, I have personally been attacked by witches and wizards that have manifested themselves as baboons or owls. Those dreams revealed what the enemy was trying to put in my **'horn'**. In my deliverance sessions in Nigeria, I have recognized Christians who were being attacked by water spirits once they inform me that they have been attacked by snakes in their dreams. Therefore, dreams can be used to determine what you have in your **'horn'** or what the devil is trying to contaminate your **'horn'** with.

How Does The 'Oil' Leak From The 'Horn'?

Our Lord Jesus Christ spells out how the *'oil'* gets drained from the *'horn'* in the parable of the sower.

MARK 4:18-19

18 "Now these are the ones sown among thorns; they are the ones who hear the word,

19 "and THE CARES OF THIS WORLD, THE DECEITFULNESS OF RICHES, and THE DESIRES FOR OTHER THINGS entering in choke the word, and it becomes unfruitful.

The more you are pre-occupied with *the cares of this world, the deceitfulness of riches, and the desires for other things,* the more cracks you have in your *'horn'* through which the *'oil'* leaks away. Since Satan is the "*god of this world*" (**2 COR. 4:4**), we exist in a world with a negative spiritual climate. As a result, there is a constant pressure on your *'horn'* to crack for the *'oil'* to leak away.

You Should Be A Flowing Stream Of 'Oil'

What happens when you have oil that is not refreshed by being poured out and replaced? What happens when you don't use the oil, but you let the oil to become stagnant? The oil gathers insects and begins to stink. In fact, there is a scripture for this:

ECCL. 10:1
1 Dead flies putrefy the perfumer's ointment *(oil).*

And cause it to give off a foul odor.

What happens when you feed on the Word, listen to tapes but do not exercise your faith? You grow spiritually fat and flabby. In other words, you should be a flowing stream and not just a cistern since stagnation makes the *'oil'* in your *'horn'* to gather flies, to rot and to stink. You are supposed to be a channel, a river, and not a cistern. The flies that die in your *'oil'* come from offense and lack of action (i.e. stagnation) in using the anointing. You stink when you don't use your anointing. Your flesh stinks when you don't use your anointing. Once you get the *'oil'*, you should pour it out immediately and get re-filled again. You must be willing to be spent for the kingdom of God. What did Paul tell Timothy in **2 TIM. 4:6?**

2 TIM. 4:6
6 For I AM ALREADY BEING POURED OUT as a drink offering and the time of my departure is at hand.

In another epistle Paul wrote:

PHIL. 2:17
17 Yes, and if I AM BEING POURED OUT as a drink offering on the sacrifice and service of your faith, I am glad and rejoice with you all.

Just like Paul, you should be willing to be poured out, to be spent for the kingdom of God and not to be a stagnant *'horn'* of *'oil'*. Be sold out and be committed to give your all for the sake of the Gospel.

Fill With Oil, Not Put Some Oil

Notice that God did not say "put *some* oil in the horn". God said "*fill* the horn with oil". That is why if you, reading this book, are just born-again but not filled with the Holy Ghost, God wants you to go to the next step. God wants you to be filled with the Holy Spirit with the evidence of speaking in other tongues. When you are just born-again, you have some *'oil'* in your *'horn'* but your *'horn'* is not filled with *'oil'*. Your *'horn'* is filled with *'oil'* when you get baptized in the Holy Ghost with the evidence of speaking with other tongues. The same Holy Ghost is involved in the *born-again* and *baptism-in-the-Holy-Ghost* experiences but they are two different experiences. Same Holy Ghost but two different experiences. In other words, the same *'oil'* but two different amounts, measures or dimensions in the two different experiences.

Further, it is insufficient to just be filled with the Holy Ghost. You are supposed to go one step further by ensuring that you are constantly full of the Holy Ghost. That is why Paul wrote passages like:

EPH. 5:18-20

18 And do not be drunk with wine, in which is dissipation; but BE FILLED WITH THE SPIRIT,

19 speaking to one another in psalms and hymns and spiritual songs, singing and making melody in your heart to the Lord, 20 giving thanks always for all things to God the Father in the name of our Lord Jesus Christ,

To be constantly full of the Holy Ghost, you have to live a lifestyle of praise and worship by *"speaking to [yourself] in psalms and hymns and spiritual songs, singing and making melody in your heart to the Lord, giving thanks always for all things to God"*. The words, *"be filled with the Spirit"* actually means *"be being filled with the Spirit"* indicating a continuous on-going action of being full and staying full of the Spirit of God. There should be constant re-fillings of the Holy Spirit by you spending a lot of time praying in tongues. You should continue to be full, everyday. Fresh re-fillings of the Holy Ghost. Fresh re-fillings of the *'oil'* of joy. You must stay full. You must remain full. Daily re-fillings of the *'oil'* of joy. Your *'horn'* should be constantly full of the *'oil'* of joy for **PROV. 15:13** says:

PROV. 15:13
13 A merry heart makes a cheerful countenance, But by sorrow of the heart the spirit is broken.

Holy Laughter

After ministering in one of the sessions of the Japanese trip that led to this book, I laid my hands on a Japanese lady to receive the baptism of the Holy Ghost. After I laid my hands on her, she fell under the power and started speaking in tongues. Before I knew what was happening, she was laughing in the spirit. As I looked at her, I picked up the holy laughter and started laughing as well. Some other Japanese Christians also started laughing in the spirit. As I was laughing in the spirit, the Lord then impressed on my heart that:

"The Japanese spiritual climate is changing.
Do not ask, 'when is the spiritual climate
going to change?' "

What is the purpose of *"holy laughter"*? *Holy laughter* helps you to release burdens. It is not just ordinary laughter. It is spiritual; it is coming from your spirit. It is like speaking in tongues. The Holy Spirit gives you utterance for holy laughter. One can laugh naturally just like one can speak naturally. But when you speak in tongues, you are speaking from your spirit. In the same way, when you laugh in the spirit, you are laughing from your spirit. When I laugh naturally, the laughter is coming from my emotions; it is coming from the soulish realm. But holy laughter is coming from your spirit. It is just like I can talk naturally from my mind, but I can only talk in tongues when I get the utterance from the Holy Ghost. You can define holy laughter as *laughter that is coming from your spirit that is given to you by the Holy Ghost*. When you are laughing in the spirit, many things happen to you spiritually, mentally and in your emotions that cannot be totally explained or put in words. What happens is that there is a great relief; you feel a refreshing. At that time, you are not hung up in terms of having all your spiritual *"i's"* dotted and *"t's"* crossed. In other words, you are not trapped in a spiritual rut of trying to be scripturally correct about every little detail in your life by the use of your own power. For example, you are not caught in a legalistic *"am I meditating on the right scripture for this situation or have I prayed enough or have I followed the ten steps for having my prayers answered?"*

You initiate holy laughter just like you initiate praying in tongues. You start by an act of your will and by stepping out in faith. First, you start in the natural, then you end up in the spiritual. The more yielded you are when you pray in tongues, the more utterance you get from the Holy Ghost and the more diverse your praying in tongues gets. It is the same way with holy laughter: the more yielded you are to the Holy Ghost, the deeper He can take you in holy laughter. Laughing in the spirit and praying in the spirit *(in tongues)* are similar: in both cases, you audibly express an utterance given to your spirit by the Holy Spirit. Therefore, I seriously doubt if you can laugh in the spirit if you are not spirit-filled with the evidence of speaking in other tongues.

Just laughing in the natural will not pour the **'oil'** of joy into your **'horn'**. It is spiritual laughter that gets the job done. When I face impossible situations or when the devil tries to tell me that I am defeated, I immediately engage in spiritual laughter. By an act of my will I step out in faith and start laughing in the natural; I finally end up laughing in the spirit. When you are tempted to be depressed, turn the whole situation around by laughing in the spirit. Re-generate the *'oil'* of joy in your *'horn'* by laughing in the spirit. You can do this anytime by a simple act of your will. Fill your *'horn'* with *'oil'* by engaging in spiritual laughter.

Importance Of Being Full For Ministry

The importance of being full for ministry is underscored by the story in **ACTS 6**.

ACTS 6:1-4
1 Now in those days, when the number of the disciples was multiplying, there arose a complaint against the Hebrews by the Hellenists, because their widows were neglected in the daily distribution.
2 Then the twelve summoned the multitude of the disciples and said, "It is not desirable that we should leave the word of God and serve tables.
3 "Therefore, brethren, seek out from among you seven men of good reputation, FULL OF THE HOLY GHOST and wisdom, whom we may appoint over this business;
4 "but WE WILL GIVE OURSELVES CONTINUALLY TO PRAYER AND TO THE MINISTRY OF THE WORD."

The apostles, in essence, said that, after *good character,* the number two qualification for those to be appointed as deacons was that their *'horns'* must be full of the *'oil'* of the Holy Ghost. Notice, they did not say they were seeking men who were just 'filled' (*past tense*) with the Holy Ghost in the sense of being baptized in the Holy Ghost with the evidence of speaking with other tongues. Back then, almost every believer was filled with the Holy Ghost with the evidence of speaking in other tongues; that was not the issue. They wanted men that were not only 'filled' (*past tense*) but that are currently ***'full'*** and that stay ***'full'*** (*present continuous tense*).

Furthermore, they refused to be distracted with the mechanics of ministry. Rather, the apostles wanted to ensure that their ***'horns'*** remained full by *"we will give ourselves continually to prayer and to the ministry of the word."* Notice that they said *"we will give ourselves"*. In other words, staying full is an act of your will and *"your flesh"* is the price you pay for staying full. God's ways are always old-fashioned. There are no short cuts and they are never on sale. The price always remains the same. There is no big secret to finding the power of God and the presence of the Holy Spirit in our lives. It comes the old fashioned way - by dedication to prayer and by dying to the flesh. *"Praying through"* means staying on your knees until you have touched heaven. In other words, staying on your knees until your ***'horn'*** is filled with fresh ***'oil'***.

You can only minister from your overflow since *"out of the abundance of the heart the mouth speaks "* (**MATT. 12:34**). It is irrelevant how busy we are for the Lord, or what kind of spiritual experiences we may have had in the past, or how much we *"intend"* to do for the Lord. The truth is if we do not nurture the presence of the Holy Spirit we will suffer the results - a life and ministry lacking His power and presence. *"Intending to pray"* or *"maintaining an attitude of prayer"* are no substitutes for praying. It doesn't matter how big or well-known your ministry is, or how *"deep"* your walk with the Lord appears to be. If we neglect time with God, our ministry suffers since our **'horns'** cannot remain full of the **'oil'** of the Holy Spirit without a life of prayer. Ministers must press on to be filled with all the fullness of God. If they refuse to be filled with all God's fullness, they will surely miss God and fail in fulfilling the ministry God has planned for them.

Let us look again at what the apostles said in **ACTS 6:2** – *"It is not desirable that we should leave the word of God and serve tables."* This statement shows the premium that the apostles placed on being full and staying full. Because of their fullness, the Bible records verses like:

ACTS 4:33

33 And with GREAT POWER, THE APOSTLES GAVE WITNESS to the resurrection of the Lord Jesus.

Stephen is another illustration of the importance of staying full for ministry.

ACTS 6:8

8 And Stephen FULL of faith and power did great wonders and signs among the people.

Every time the Bible talks about Stephen, the Bible says Stephen was full. Stephen was able to do *great wonders and signs among the people* because he was *full* of faith and power. He was full of power because he was full of the Holy Ghost. He was full of faith because he was full of the Word since faith comes by hearing the Word of God (**ROM. 10:17**). You can certainly see that he was full of the Word when you observe that he quoted from heart scripture after scripture from **ACTS 7:2** to **ACTS 7:50** in his defense before the high priest and the council. See the way the Word was gushing out of Stephen's full *'horn'* in **ACTS 7:2-50**!

ACTS 7:2-50

2 And he *(STEPHEN)* **said, "Brethren and fathers, listen: The God of glory appeared to our father Abraham when he was in Mesopotamia, before he dwelt in Haran,**

3 and said to him, 'Get out of your country and from your relatives, and come to a land that I will show you.'

4 Then he came out of the land of the Chaldeans and dwelt in Haran. And from there, when his father was dead, He moved him to this land in which you now dwell.

5 And *God* **gave him no inheritance in it, not even** *enough* **to set his foot on. But even when** *Abraham* **had no child, He promised to give it to him for a possession, and to his descendants after him.**

6 But God spoke in this way: that his descendants would dwell in a foreign land, and that they would bring them into bondage and oppress *them* four hundred years.

7 'And the nation to whom they will be in bondage I will judge,' said God, 'and after that they shall come out and serve Me in this place.'

8 Then He gave him the covenant of circumcision; and so *Abraham* begot Isaac and circumcised him on the eighth day; and Isaac *begot* Jacob, and Jacob *begot* the twelve patriarchs.

9 "And the patriarchs, becoming envious, sold Joseph into Egypt. But God was with him

10 and delivered him out of all his troubles, and gave him favor and wisdom in the presence of Pharaoh, king of Egypt; and he made him governor over Egypt and all his house.

11 Now a famine and great trouble came over all the land of Egypt and Canaan, and our fathers found no sustenance.

12 But when Jacob heard that there was grain in Egypt, he sent out our fathers first.

13 And the second *time* Joseph was made known to his brothers, and Joseph's family became known to the Pharaoh.

14 Then Joseph sent and called his father Jacob and all his relatives to *him,* seventy-five people.

15 So Jacob went down to Egypt; and he died, he and our fathers.

16 And they were carried back to Shechem and laid in the tomb that Abraham bought for a sum of money from the sons of Hamor, *the father* of Shechem.

17 "But when the time of the promise drew near which God had sworn to Abraham, the people grew and multiplied in Egypt

18 till another king arose who did not know Joseph.

19 This man dealt treacherously with our people, and oppressed our forefathers, making them expose their babies, so that they might not live.

20 At this time Moses was born, and was well pleasing to God; and he was brought up in his father's house for three months.

21 But when he was set out, Pharaoh's daughter took him away and brought him up as her own son.

22 And Moses was learned in all the wisdom of the Egyptians, and was mighty in words and deeds.

23 "Now when he was forty years old, it came into his heart to visit his brethren, the children of Israel.

24 And seeing one of *them* suffer wrong, he defended and avenged him who was oppressed, and struck down the Egyptian.

25 For he supposed that his brethren would have understood that God would deliver them by his hand, but they did not understand.

26 And the next day he appeared to *two of* them as they were fighting, and *tried to* reconcile them, saying, 'Men, you are brethren; why do you wrong one another?'

27 But he who did his neighbor wrong pushed him away, saying, 'Who made you a ruler and a judge over us?

28 Do you want to kill me as you did the Egyptian yesterday?'

29 Then, at this saying, Moses fled and became a dweller in the land of Midian, where he had two sons.

30 "And when forty years had passed, an Angel of the Lord appeared to him in a flame of fire in a bush, in the wilderness of Mount Sinai.

31 When Moses saw *it,* he marveled at the sight; and as he drew near to observe, the voice of the Lord came to him,

32 *saying,* 'I *am* the God of your fathers—the God of Abraham, the God of Isaac, and the God of Jacob.' And Moses trembled and dared not look.

33 'Then the LORD SAID TO HIM, "TAKE YOUR SANDALS OFF YOUR FEET, FOR THE PLACE WHERE YOU STAND IS HOLY GROUND.

34 I HAVE SURELY SEEN THE OPPRESSION OF MY PEOPLE WHO ARE IN EGYPT; I HAVE HEARD THEIR GROANING AND HAVE COME DOWN TO DELIVER THEM. AND NOW COME, I WILL SEND YOU TO EGYPT."'

35 "THIS MOSES WHOM THEY REJECTED, SAYING, 'WHO MADE YOU A RULER AND A JUDGE?' IS THE ONE GOD SENT *to be* a ruler and a deliverer by the hand of the Angel who appeared to him in the bush.

36 He brought them out, after he had shown wonders and signs in the land of Egypt, and in the Red Sea, and in the wilderness forty years.

Israel Rebels Against God

37 "This is that Moses who said to the children of Israel, 'The LORD YOUR GOD WILL RAISE UP FOR YOU A PROPHET LIKE ME FROM YOUR BRETHREN. HIM YOU SHALL HEAR.'

38 "This is he who was in the congregation in the wilderness with the Angel who spoke to him on Mount Sinai, and *with* our fathers, the one who received the living oracles to give to us,

39 whom our fathers would not obey, but rejected. And in their hearts they turned back to Egypt,

40 saying to Aaron, 'Make us gods to go before us; *as for* this Moses who brought us out of the land of Egypt, we do not know what has become of him.'

41 And they made a calf in those days, offered sacrifices to the idol, and rejoiced in the works of their own hands.

42 Then God turned and gave them up to worship the host of heaven, as it is written in the book of the Prophets:

'Did you offer Me slaughtered animals and sacrifices *during* forty years in the wilderness,

O house of Israel?

43 You also took up the tabernacle of Moloch,

And the star of your god Remphan,

Images which you made to worship;

And I will carry you away beyond Babylon.'

God's True Tabernacle

44 "Our fathers had the tabernacle of witness in the wilderness, as He appointed, instructing Moses to make it according to the pattern that he had seen,

45 which our fathers, having received it in turn, also brought with Joshua into the land possessed by the Gentiles, whom God drove out before the face of our fathers until the days of David,

46 who found favor before God and asked to find a dwelling for the God of Jacob.

47 But Solomon built Him a house.

48 "However, the Most High does not dwell in temples made with hands, as the prophet says:

49 'Heaven *is* My throne,

And earth *is* My footstool.

What house will you build for Me? says the LORD,

Or what *is* the place of My rest?

50 Has My hand not made all these things?

Re-Filling Your 'Horn" After Ministering

If you are a minister, you should be mindful of the fact that, after ministering, your *'horn'* is drained because the *'oil'* has been poured out. You are then like a discharged battery that has to be re-charged. Ministers should realize that, yes, some of their tiredness after ministering is naturally based because some physical energy was expended while ministering. However, some of the tiredness is spiritually based. That is why not all the tiredness after ministering goes away by just resting physically. For all the tiredness to go away, you must take care of the spiritual aspect. Therefore, after ministering I do rest physically, but I don't rest spiritually. Rather, I ensure that I re-fill my *'horn'* immediately with fresh *'oil'* by reading many Bible chapters and listening to many tapes of other preachers.

Earthen Vessels Crack And Leak

2 COR. 4:7-8
7 But we have this TREASURE IN EARTHEN VESSELS, that the excellence of the power may be of God and not of us.
8 *We are* **hard-pressed on every side, yet not crushed;**

Paul likens our *'horns'* to earthen vessels. But earthen vessels crack, leak and are porous since we live in a negative world. Therefore, to prevent empty *'horns'* there must be constant refilling with the Word of God and constant renewals of the spirit. The fact that Paul ensured that his *'horn'* was always full was the reason why Paul's *'horn'* was never *crushed* even though he was *"hard-pressed on every side"* **(2 COR. 4:8).** If you want to obtain Paul's results, do what Paul did: always keep your *'horn'* full of the Word and the Spirit.

Being Filled, Was Led

If you read the New Testament carefully, you will notice that the emphasis is on first, the believer has to constantly be filled with the Word of God, second, the believer has to constantly be filled with the Spirit, and third, the believer has to constantly be led by the Spirit.

LUKE 4:1

1 Then Jesus, BEING FILLED WITH THE HOLY SPIRIT, returned from the Jordan and WAS LED BY THE SPIRIT ...

Jesus, *"being filled with the Holy Spirit was led."* Similarly, it is much easier to be led by the Spirit if your *'horn'* is full of *'oil'* (that is full of the Spirit).

Being Filled, Speaking

EPH. 5:18-19

18 And do not be drunk with wine, in which is dissipation; but BE FILLED WITH THE SPIRIT,

19 SPEAKING TO ONE ANOTHER IN PSALMS AND HYMNS AND SPIRITUAL SONGS, SINGING AND MAKING MELODY IN YOUR HEART TO THE LORD,

20 giving thanks always for all things to God the Father in the name of our Lord Jesus Christ,

The words, *"be filled with the Spirit"* actually are *"be being filled with the Spirit"* denoting a constant re-filling of the Spirit. Notice that once you are full, you will speak. Once your *'horn'* is full of *'oil'*, the *'oil'* will spill over the brim of your *'horn'*. The spirit-filled believer who is constantly being filled with the Spirit will be noticed as *"psalms, hymns, spiritual songs"* will be gushing out from his full *'horn'*. The *"psalms, hymns, spiritual songs"* are a source of great joy and refreshing. Therefore, the believer who has a full *'horn'* does not need any counterfeit joy or buzz from any alcoholic beverage.

COL. 3:15-16

15 And let the peace of God rule in your hearts, to which also you were called in one body; and be thankful.
16 Let the WORD OF CHRIST DWELL IN YOU RICHLY in all wisdom, TEACHING AND ADMONISHING ONE ANOTHER IN PSALMS AND HYMNS AND SPIRITUAL SONGS, SINGING with grace in your hearts to the Lord.

Paul conveyed the same concepts to the churches even though he may have used different words. The phrase, *"word of Christ dwell in you richly"* means your *'horn'* should be filled with the Word of God. The result of your *'horn'* being full of the Word of God is that you will be able to *"teach and admonish one another in psalms and hymns and spiritual songs, singing with grace in your hearts to the Lord."*

Chapter 6
"FILL YOUR HORN WITH OIL AND GO"

Weeping or grieving is scriptural and natural. Jesus Himself wept (**JN. 11:35**). David wept after the loss of his family and belongings at Ziklag (**1 SAM. 30:5**). Trying to be macho, I did not grieve when my dad died when I was 17 years. My not grieving at the appropriate time bothered me ten years later when I was 27 years.

ECCL. 3:4

4 A time to weep,

And a time to laugh;

A time to mourn,

And a time to dance;

It is perfectly fine to grieve. But according to **ECCL. 3:4** above, there is a time to stop weeping. There is a time to stop weeping, "*fill your horn with oil and go*". David stopped at some point and re-generated his anointing (*David strengthened himself in the Lord his God* -**1 SAM. 30:6**). After filling his '*horn*' with '*oil*', David then went to recover his wives and belongings. It was natural for Samuel to grieve for Saul. But after a reasonable time of grieving, God, in essence, said, *"enough of the grieving, now get up, re-generate the anointing and go do something about the situation."*

God Anoints You For Somebody Else

Benny Hinn once said, *"God has another person in mind, when He anoints you."* This is in line with certain statements made by Paul to the Ephesians.

EPH. 3:2
2 If indeed you have heard of the dispensation of the GRACE OF GOD WHICH WAS GIVEN ME FOR YOU.

In other words, Paul said *"I was anointed for you."* This explains why healing evangelists can have sicknesses in their bodies if they don't know how to appropriate healing for themselves by applying the Word of God. They cannot just automatically apply the healing anointing in their ministries to themselves since the anointing is for somebody else. In the same way, a prophet cannot just automatically switch on the prophetic ministry to obtain guidance regarding his own personal affairs. Rather, the prophet has to follow the inward witness like any other christian when it has to do with his personal issues. The anointing is no one's personal property. Just as God told Samuel to go and anoint David, God wants you to go and use the *'oil'* in your *'horn'* to bless somebody else.

Go

God did not tell Samuel *"fill your horn with oil and stay"*. God told Samuel *"fill your horn with oil and go"*. John Osteen once said *"Two-thirds of **GOD's** name is 'GO'."* The anointing always calls for outreach. The anointing is always meant for an outward-going action to bless somebody else. Just as God told Samuel to *"**fill his horn and GO"*** anoint David to be king of Israel, God is telling you today to *"fill you horn and GO"* and anoint somebody else to fulfill his destiny as king over his own circumstances. In the Great Commission (**MATT. 28:18-20; MARK 16:15-18**), the Lord Jesus Christ gave us both the commandment and the equipment to fulfill the commandment.

MATT. 28:18-20
18 And Jesus came and spoke to them, saying, "All authority has been given to Me in heaven and on earth.
19 GO therefore and make disciples of all the nations, baptizing them in the name of the Father and of the Son and of the Holy Spirit,
20 teaching them to observe all things that I have commanded you; and lo, I am with you always, even to the end of the age." Amen.

MARK 16:15-18
15 And He said to them, "GO into all the world and preach the gospel to every creature.
16 He who believes and is baptized will be saved; but he who does not believe will be condemned.

17 And these signs will follow those who believe: In My name they will cast out demons; they will speak with new tongues; 18 they will take up serpents; and if they drink anything deadly, it will by no means hurt them; they will lay hands on the sick, and they will recover."

In other words, He did not just send us out with empty *'horns'* but has also provided the *'oil'* in the person of the Holy Spirit. Now is the time to declare the glorious gospel! Hearts are open to hear the truth. By the millions they will turn to the Lord, if we will only be faithful to take every opportunity to share Jesus with those that are hurting. Each of us has a job to do in this end-time harvest. We must spend time in prayer and in the Word to get our *'horns'* full of the *'oil'* of the Holy Ghost. After getting our *'horns'* full of the *'oil'*, we are to *GO* and carry out the Great Commission.

Stir Yourself Up

Paul told Timothy:

2 TIM. 1:6

6 ... STIR UP the gift of God which is in you through the laying on of my hands.

2 TIM. 4:2

2 BE READY in season and out of season.

In other words, Paul told Timothy *"rekindle the gift and remain stirred up at all times."* That is, you have to have your *'horn'* full at all times, whether you like it or not. Samuel certainly did not feel like filling his *'horn'* and going that day God told him to **"fill your horn and go"** but he had to do it anyway. The following kinds of thoughts could have run through Samuel's mind on that day: *"How am I sure that the next king will not fail just as Saul failed? After all, God had told the people of Israel that their having a king was not His perfect will for them."* In spite of those kinds of thoughts, Samuel had to **fill his horn and go** anyway. You are supposed to be filling your *'horn'* and going every single day and every single time.

Be Ready To Be Poured Out

In **ACTS 15:26**, the apostles in Jerusalem commended Paul and Barnabas for totally selling out to the preaching of the gospel.

ACTS 15:25-26
25 It seemed good to us, being assembled with one accord, to send chosen men to you with our beloved BARNABAS AND PAUL,
26 MEN WHO HAVE RISKED THEIR LIVES FOR THE NAME OF OUR LORD JESUS CHRIST.

In the Old Testament, drink offerings were poured on altars (e.g. **2 KINGS 16:13** – ... *he poured his drink offering ... on the altar.*)

Having this picture of the Old Testament sacrifice as a backdrop, Paul wrote:

PHIL. 2:17

17 Yes, and if I AM BEING POURED OUT as a drink offering on the sacrifice and service of your faith, I am glad and rejoice with you all.

2 TIM. 4:6

6 For I AM ALREADY BEING POURED OUT as a drink offering and the time of my departure is at hand.

2 COR. 12:15

15 And I will very gladly spend and be spent for your souls;

Paul gave his all for the ministry. He repeatedly poured himself out to those he was ministering to. This represented his earnestness, his zeal, his total willingness to be used, to be spent and to be poured out to those he came in contact with. In the context of this book, imagine yourself as a *'horn'* that is filled with *'oil'* to be poured out. For the sake of the gospel, be ready to be poured out. After being filled, go out and be poured out to help somebody else. Come back, get filled again, go again and be poured out again.

Cannot Tell What Is In The Horn Until You Pour The Oil Out

Elisha did not know the potential in Elijah's mantle that dropped on him until he struck the waters after saying, *"Where is the LORD God of Elijah?"* (**2 KINGS 2:14**). In the same way, you do not know what gift you have in your *'horn'* until you act in faith. You must act.

Smith Wigglesworth once told a man, *"the Acts of the Apostles would never have been written if the apostles had not acted."* Samuel did not know the limitless possibilities represented by the *'oil'* that he poured on David. For example, the anointing represented by that *'oil'* enabled David to slay Goliath and to make him one of the greatest kings in the history of Israel. You do not know what you have in your *'horn'* until you pour the *'oil'* out.

Who/What Is Your 'Saul'?

What does *'Saul'* represent? Your *'Saul'* is all your failed dreams, all your disappointments. Your *'Saul'* is: ***"I have tried this approach in ministry and it did not work. I have tried this pastor and this pastor failed me. I have tried this church and this church failed me."*** Your *'Saul'* represents the '**who**' or '**what**' on which you have wasted your efforts, squandered your anointing, or poured your *'oil'* without any harvest in return.

Forgetting Those Things Which Are Behind

PHIL. 3:13-14

13 Brethren, I do not count myself to have apprehended; but one thing *I do,* **FORGETTING THOSE THINGS WHICH ARE BEHIND and reaching forward to those things which are ahead,
14 I PRESS TOWARD THE GOAL for the prize of the upward call of God in Christ Jesus.**

Paul had many reasons to forget the past. One major reason is that several ministers disappointed Paul. For example, Demas was one of the *'Sauls'* Paul had to forget. In **PHILEMON 24**, we read about Demas being with Paul earlier.

PHILE. 23-24

**23 Epaphras, my fellow prisoner in Christ Jesus, greets you,
24** *as do* **Mark, Aristarchus, DEMAS, Luke, my fellow laborers.**

But in **2 TIMOTHY**, Paul urged Timothy to come quickly since Demas had forsaken him!

2 TIM. 4:9-10

**9 Be diligent to come to me quickly;
10 FOR DEMAS HAS FORSAKEN ME, having loved this present world, and has departed for Thessalonica**

Because of *'Sauls'* like Demas that fell from grace, Paul had to *"forget those things which are behind and press toward the goal"*. In other words, Paul had to **"Fill his horn with oil and go!"**

Fill Your Horn With Oil And Go!

Are you dejected because you are facing the same situation as Joshua whose spiritual father, Moses, has just passed away?
"Fill your horn with oil and go!"

Are you dejected because you are facing the same situation as Samuel whose spiritual son, Saul, has just fallen from grace?
"Fill your horn with oil and go!"

Are you dejected because you are facing the same situation as Elisha whose spiritual son, Gehazi, has just failed him after he had invested so much in him?
"Fill your horn with oil and go!"

Are you dejected because your pastor or your favorite TV evangelist has just fallen into sexual sin? We are to *"follow people [only] as they follow Christ"* **(1 COR. 11:1)**.
Therefore,

"Fill your horn with oil and go!"

Are you disappointed in ministry or disappointed for any reason? Do not let your disappointment lead to discouragement, depression and oppression.

"Fill your horn with oil and go!"

Have you just lost a loved one?

"Fill your horn with oil and go!"

Are you so discouraged that you don't even want to get up from bed?

"Fill your horn with oil and go!"

Do you lack motivation to go to work because you have been unjustly denied the promotion that you deserve?

"Fill your horn with oil and go!"

The reason why **1 SAM. 16:1** made such an impression on me as I was flying to Japan in 2000 was because I had just been greatly disappointed. Just before leaving for Japan in 2000, a crusade engagement I had planned with a Japanese pastor had just been cancelled. That was not the first time my crusade plans for Japan had been scuttled. Therefore, I was naturally dejected. The disappointment was weighing my spirit down. I needed all the encouragement the Holy Spirit could offer. Hence, it was appropriate when, as I was airborne on that Japan Airlines plane, sitting between a Japanese man and a Japanese woman, God encouraged me with **1 SAM. 16:1** – "**Fill your horn with oil and go!**"

APPENDIX I
SINNER'S PRAYER TO RECEIVE JESUS CHRIST AS SAVIOR

✝

If you have never been born again, I want to encourage you to sincerely pray the following prayer:

Dear Heavenly Father,

I repent and turn away from sin. In your Word, **ROMANS 10:9-10** says: **"that if you confess with your mouth the Lord Jesus and believe in your heart that God has raised Him from the dead, you will be saved. For with the heart one believes unto righteousness, and with the mouth confession is made unto salvation."**

I believe in my heart that Jesus Christ is the Son of God. I believe that God has raised Him from the dead for my justification. And now, I confess Him as my Lord. Lord, thank you for my salvation!

Now, you are born again if you have sincerely prayed the above prayer. In order to grow spiritually, join a Bible-based church and read your Bible everyday starting with the Gospel of John. I also encourage you to pray the next prayer to receive the baptism in the Holy Spirit with the evidence **of speaking in other tongues.**

APPENDIX II
A BELIEVER'S PRAYER TO RECEIVE THE BAPTISM IN THE HOLY SPIRIT WITH THE EVIDENCE OF SPEAKING IN OTHER TONGUES

If you are born-again but you have never been baptized in the Holy Spirit with the evidence of speaking in other tongues, I want to encourage you to pray the following prayer:

Dear Heavenly Father,

In your Word, **LUKE 11:13** says: **"If you then being evil know how to give good gifts to your children, how much more will your heavenly Father give the Holy Spirit to those who ask Him!"**

I am asking You to fill me with the Holy Spirit. Dear Holy Spirit, rise up within me as I praise God. I fully expect to speak with other tongues as You give me the utterance **(ACTS 2:4).**

Now, begin to praise God for filling you with the Holy Spirit. Speak the words you receive –not in your own language, but in the language given to you by the Holy Spirit. It is you that has to speak in other tongues; the Holy Spirit will not force you to speak in other tongues. Worship and praise God in your heavenly language – in other tongues.

www.ingramcontent.com/pod-product-compliance
Ingram Content Group UK Ltd.
Pitfield, Milton Keynes, MK11 3LW, UK
UKHW041955230426
12048UKWH00008B/346